THE YEAR OF THE BIBLE

LEADER'S MANUAL

THE YEAR OF THE BIBLE
A COMPREHENSIVE, CONGREGATION-WIDE PROGRAM OF BIBLE READING

JAMES E. DAVISON

THE *WHOLE* BIBLE
DURING THE *WHOLE* YEAR
WITH THE *WHOLE* CONGREGATION

BRIDGE RESOURCES
LOUISVILLE, KENTUCKY

© 1996 James E. Davison

All rights reserved. No part of this publication may be reproduced in any form or by any means without permission in writing from the publisher.

Scripture quotations in this publication are from the New Revised Standard Version of the Bible, copyright © 1989 by the Division of Christian Education of the National Council of the Churches of Christ in the U.S.A. Used by permission.

The schedule of readings for *The Year of the Bible* originally appeared in *Daily Devotions: Encounters with God* and *Discovery* and is reprinted by permission from Scripture Union, P.O. Box 6720, Wayne, PA 19087.

Additional copies of this book and other materials for *The Year of the Bible* may be obtained by calling 1-800-524-2612.

Book design by Anthony Feltner
Cover design by Anthony Feltner
Edited by Beth Basham

First edition

Published by Bridge Resources
Louisville, Kentucky

PRINTED IN THE UNITED STATES OF AMERICA

To the Members of

Westminster Presbyterian Church

Upper St. Clair, Pennsylvania

with thanks

CONTENTS

Acknowledgments	ix
Introduction: *The Year of the Bible*	1
The Value of the Program	3
Making the Program Work	6
Chapter 1	
Getting Going: Planning for the Program	9
Gaining Support	9
Developing Plans	13
Projecting Your Costs	18
Chapter 2	
Starting Up: Inaugurating the Year	21
Publicizing the Program	21
Instituting the Year	24
Chapter 3	
The Long Haul: Maintaining Enthusiasm	29
Regular Features	30
Additional Possibilities	33
Chapter 4	
Wrapping Up: Concluding the Program	41
Closing Activities	41
Follow-up Plans	46
Appendix 1	
Sample Materials for *The Year of the Bible*	51
Appendix 2	
Weekly Bulletin Questions	63

ACKNOWLEDGMENTS

For years I have believed that knowledge of the Scriptures is a crucial element in the life of a faithful congregation. Finding a way to increase the general level of biblical knowledge in a congregation, however, is difficult. A whole variety of factors in contemporary society—from competing activities to short attention spans to spectator-sport attitudes—stand in the way of raising the level of biblical literacy effectively.

There are many approaches to Bible study, and I suspect that there is no one best way for every person, every congregation, and every situation. Probably a combination of approaches will have the best effect in the long run. In that vein, I offer *The Year of the Bible* as one way to work toward a solution to the problem. While the program stands on its own, it is compatible with a variety of other approaches, and it can be coordinated with a congregation's overarching program of Christian education.

The value of *The Year of the Bible* is that it can focus the attention of a congregation on the Scriptures for an entire year. This has been confirmed for me by my own experience in developing the program originally for Westminster Presbyterian Church in Upper St. Clair, a suburb of Pittsburgh, Pennsylvania, and then subsequently in working with the Committee on Worship and Theology of Pittsburgh Presbytery to conduct a presbytery-wide "Year of the Bible" in 1995, in which eighty-five congregations participated. Not only does the program enable those who participate to expand their knowledge of the Bible as a whole, but it also stimulates their interest and enthusiasm for the Scriptures.

Acknowledgments provide an opportunity to thank those who have been especially helpful in developing an idea into a finished product. Many people have been helpful to me, of course. First of all, I want to thank the members of Westminster for their participation and support. It is to them that this book is dedicated.

A number of members encouraged me to pursue the original idea for a study of the "Year of the Bible" in 1988. Others aided me with planning and implementation. The officers of the congregation not only endorsed the program, but signed on the dotted line themselves when I asked for their pledge to take part. (You will see the specifics of what they agreed to do in the sample resolution in chapter one.) Then, after I had received requests from other pastors and educators to use the program in their own congregations, I sent out a call to our members for help in organizing a "Year of the Bible" for Pittsburgh Presbytery in 1995. About thirty-five members volunteered their services and helped in various ways over a twenty-one month period as we organized and conducted the program. My thanks to all will have to be summarized by mentioning the names of those who coordinated various aspects of the project: Howard Oliver, Patricia Hurlbert, Della Inman, David Inman, David Hilty, and Ginger Parmalee.

While I cannot list the names of all those who provided me with suggestions and ideas along the way, I do want to thank a number of individuals who have encouraged and supported me. Rev. Donald Griggs and

ACKNOWLEDGMENTS

Patricia Griggs, Rev. Arthur van Eck, Mrs. Vera White, and the Revs. Carleton and Elinor Stock. My thanks also go to the members of the Committee on Worship and Theology of Pittsburgh Presbytery, who sponsored this project and helped in various ways. In addition, I wish to express my gratitude to those who were part of the program staff of Westminster Presbyterian Church of Pittsburgh, Pennsylvania, during the initial program, for without their encouragement and endorsement, *The Year of the Bible* could not have become a congregation-wide event in the first place. Thanks to the ministers, Laird Stuart, Emory Lowe, and Glen Hallead, and to the Director of Music, Walter Horsley, for their support! Special thanks go to three people who have served as my secretary at different stages of this project, Karen Richards, Elsie Hall, and Sandy Conley. Not only their secretarial skills and good ideas, but also their friendship and advice have been a great blessing to me along the way. Would that everyone had the great good fortune to work with such capable and caring people!

Finally, a word of thanks, too, goes to my family: to my wife, Reeny, for her continual support and her encouragement to keep at it, and to my children, Tim, Andrew, and Scott, whose active lives reminded me (especially when I was "keeping at it" particularly intensively) of another primary responsibility of the Christian life—to spend time with your family.

James E. Davison

INTRODUCTION

Many people say that twentieth-century Christians are "biblically illiterate." While this is certainly not true of all individuals, it is apparent that many church members today do not know the Bible very well. This is an unfortunate state of affairs, particularly for those denominations, like my own, that have traditionally placed a premium on knowledge of the Scriptures. Whatever the denomination, however, this is unfortunate for an even more significant reason: the Bible is the basis of our faith. As God's written Word for us, it communicates the knowledge of Christ and God's will for our lives.

You may have wondered, as I have, what can be done to reverse the tide. How can we help people in our congregations begin to learn the Scriptures—to become comfortable with them, to understand their basic themes, and to apply them in their daily lives? Bible study groups can be of help. In-depth Bible courses can help too. Oftentimes, however, such attempts reach only a few people. Generally, it is those people who have been in a number of Bible studies who sign up for new ones when they are offered. What can we do to effect a major breakthrough in the level of biblical literacy in a large portion of a congregation within a relatively brief period of time?

This book outlines a program that will generate a high level of enthusiasm for reading the Bible on a regular basis, and it will do that in a broad cross-section of your congregation. I first developed the idea in 1988 at Westminster Presbyterian Church, in Pittsburgh, Pennsylvania. Since then, it has been employed by over 100 congregations in the Western Pennsylvania area and around the country. Basically, the program is quite simple. It centers on a challenge to the whole congregation to read the entire Bible in one year, and it builds an extensive program that involves the total life of the congregation around that effort.

In the process of designing the program, I discovered that people really do want to know the Bible better. The desire may be unconscious, but people in our pews appear to have a deep thirst to understand the Scriptures more fully. My experience has been that if you give people the chance to read the Scriptures and if you offer them help in doing so, they will seize the opportunity.

Although the original intention of *The Year of the Bible* was to motivate members who hardly knew the Scriptures to read the Bible, I have been pleased to discover that the program is equally attractive to people who are already well acquainted with the Scriptures. The reason for the broad appeal of this particular program is that it is truly comprehensive.

The Year of the Bible encompasses a number of interrelated elements:

- It centers on the whole Bible. Those who participate will experience the entire panorama of biblical history as they read the whole of the Scriptures.
- It challenges the whole congregation. The program provides an

INTRODUCTION

opportunity that all members can undertake together regardless of differing levels of biblical knowledge.

- It incorporates the congregation's entire life together. The program offers a focal point for the congregation, allowing a church to tie together all the various elements of its life, such as worship services, sermons, Bible studies, daily devotions, retreats, and so forth.
- It spans the entire year. The core of the program is a plan of daily readings that divides the material into roughly equal segments. Since each participant receives a brochure outlining the materials, it is easy for people to keep track of where they are in their readings.

All of these elements combine to make this program a unified, coherent whole. Thus, if you are looking for a program that offers a systematic and structural way to increase your congregation's familiarity with the Scriptures, you will find the program outlined in this book to be immensely helpful.

THE VALUE OF THE PROGRAM

At various times, people have spoken to me about the impact that participating in *The Year of the Bible* has had on their lives. The following statements will give you an idea of how members of Westminster Church have reacted to the program:

"When I finished the readings, I felt this was one of the most outstanding accomplishments of my life. Now several months have passed, and the pervasiveness of the Word has become intensely personal. So many things in life make sense!"

"This year of reading and study has really been a great learning experience and a wonderful discipline."

"Reading the Bible in its entirety is something I have always wanted to do. That was a motivating factor, as was knowing that others were reading (and talking about) the same passages throughout the year."

Westminster is a large congregation numbering some 2,500 members. It is typical of many North American suburban churches in the sense that members participate in a host of nonchurch activities in their businesses, communities, schools, and social lives. There is very little social pressure for members to take part in congregational programs or projects that do not appeal to them strongly. In fact, the many demands made on members' time and energy are often so great that they must pass up activities that do interest them. Nevertheless, when I first suggested the idea of *The Year of the Bible* program, people were highly enthusiastic about the proposal.

Why are people attracted to such a large-scale, time-consuming commitment? There are a number of reasons. First, people are motivated by a challenge. Or, to reverse this statement, it takes a challenge to motivate people. Apparently, people are more inclined to take on tasks and projects they otherwise might not begin, if some sort of commitment is involved. Thus, the challenge to commit themselves to this project is crucial to its success.

Second, the congregation-wide scope of the program is intriguing to people. They seem to be more interested in becoming involved when they know that others—preferably friends and acquaintances—are engaged in the same program. This sense of connectedness with others is summed up well by one person who commented, "It's exciting to know that others may be reading the exact same passage just when I am reading it."

Third, many people feel a certain amount of regret about their lack of knowledge of the Scriptures. For them, this is a welcome opportunity to read the Bible, something that they would probably not undertake on their own. When offered the chance to participate in such a program, they are aware that at the end of the year they will be able to say, "Maybe I don't know the Bible very well, but at least I've read the whole book."

Fourth, the program offers people a clear and systematic approach to acquiring a higher level of biblical literacy. Rather than thinking, "I ought to know the Bible better," and feeling at a loss as to what to do about it, they recognize an opportunity to take concrete steps toward remedying their lack of biblical knowledge.

INTRODUCTION

Fifth, and finally, perhaps the most profound reason is that many people feel that their spiritual lives are not as fulfilling as they would like them to be. Since the Scriptures are God's Word, it is obvious that reading and knowing the Scriptures are extremely important elements in experiencing a deeper spiritual life. Sensing this, people desire to know the Bible better not simply as an intellectual exercise but as a way to come closer to the Lord their God.

I suspect that people in many congregations share such feelings. *The Year of the Bible* provides an especially attractive program to tie into these needs so that people are able to achieve a specific, clear-cut, and useful goal.

Since this program works so easily and effectively in a diverse, large-church setting like Westminster, I am convinced that it will function well in most congregations. The program may be even more effective in smaller congregations, where outside pressures may not be as great and where ties to the church community tend to be stronger. In addition, because the primary thrust of the program is simply to read the Bible and to orient the life of a congregation around the readings for the year, the program promises to function effectively in churches of various denominations as well as in churches in different countries.

A word of caution is necessary, however. It is important to remember that *The Year of the Bible* is a program that will require diligent effort throughout the entire year. It will demand hard work from those who commit themselves to completing the readings, and it will necessitate even more work from those who supervise the program. Among other things, as leader you will need to continually encourage those who are participating to keep up with the program. Nevertheless, the work is well worth the effort. For many people, you will be providing a once-in-a-lifetime opportunity. For your church, you will be offering a memorable year-long experience.

Because of this experience, you can anticipate seeing the following kinds of results in your congregation:

- People who hardly know the Scriptures will find a whole new world opening up to them. They will be inspired to continue their reading of the Bible after the program has concluded.

- Those who know the Bible relatively well will find that they have gained a broader overall picture of the history of Israel, the life of Jesus Christ, and the story of the early church.
- Participants will acquire a greater awareness of the significance of the Bible for their congregation as a whole. This project is a kind of "consciousness-raising" experience. It will reaffirm how central the Scriptures are to Christian life and worship.
- People will also develop a stronger sense of oneness with others in the church. Because so many people are participating in this challenge, there will be an underlying unifying effect within the congregation as a whole.

As you can see, *The Year of the Bible* has great potential for stimulating growth and renewal in your congregation. Not only individual members, but also the congregation as a whole will benefit from joining in the program.

MAKING THE PROGRAM WORK

What will you need to do to start *The Year of the Bible* program in your congregation? First, you need to interest—and excite—the leadership of the congregation. I am thinking here not only of pastors, but also of educators, musicians, governing boards, and especially significant committees in the life of your congregation. Their enthusiastic support and endorsement are essential for the program to succeed.

Second, you will need to develop enthusiasm within the membership as a whole. This means that the idea needs to be presented well in advance so that people have the opportunity to become comfortable with it. They will need time to prepare for the project. In other words, you must bring it to their attention well before the beginning of the year that you have scheduled for the program.

INTRODUCTION

Third, you will need to find someone to spearhead the entire effort. Someone will have to see to it that the program develops smoothly. This person will nurture the project along during the entire twelve months. Probably this will be you!

You may be a pastor or a Christian educator. You may teach a church school class or be another leader in the life of your congregation. It does not really matter what your precise capacity is, because this manual contains all the resources needed to carry out *The Year of the Bible* in your congregation. Included are schedules, plans, and other written materials, along with instructions for tailoring them to your congregation.

You will also discover suggestions about some things to emphasize and some pitfalls to avoid. As a result, with a reasonable amount of effort, you can implement the program in your church in an organized and effective fashion. In addition, there are suggestions to help you sustain the program's momentum so that its impact can continue in your congregation after the year concludes.

To get an overview of the structure of *The Year of the Bible* program, I recommend that you read through the first four chapters of this book. Spend some time glancing at the materials that are provided, so that you will gain a better sense of the whole. Then you will be ready to begin developing your own plans in earnest.

It is important to develop a strategy early on, outlining how you will proceed. Next, enlist the support of a few persons whose backing will be crucial to the success of the project. When these initial steps have been taken, you will be on your way. Best wishes as you set about implementing *The Year of the Bible* in your congregation!

CHAPTER 1
GETTING GOING: PLANNING FOR THE PROGRAM

GAINING SUPPORT

This first step is the most crucial one of all. An intensive effort like this, which is intended to reach a broad range of the church members, will need the enthusiastic support of an equally broad range of the leadership of the congregation. In many ways, it is these people who will inspire others to join the project when you announce it to the congregation at large. Without their excitement, your call for a commitment to read the entire Bible in one year is likely to sound like an unattractive burden rather than a unique opportunity.

There is another reason for the importance of gaining support. You will need the help of a number of people to sustain the program throughout the year. The larger the congregation, the more you will find this to be true. In a multiple-staff church, you will need the active support of each of the ministers to provide stimulus in their own areas of responsibility. Of course, the governing board of the congregation must be behind the effort. In addition, you will probably want to enlist the backing of a number of other people who, in one way or another, hold leadership roles.

How you go about securing support will depend on your own style as well as on the makeup of the congregation. Develop a list of those individuals and groups with whom you want to share the idea. Then begin talking about the possibilities for *The Year of the Bible* with them. Discuss the basic philosophy along with some of the specifics of the program. Suggest that they read sections of this book. Explain how the project will benefit your congregation and offer them an opportunity to participate in planning the program.

The chart "Groups and Individuals to Contact" (Sample A, Appendix 1) will help you select the various people and groups who should be contacted. As you meet with people, keep a record of any suggestions that come to the fore. You will find that a number of these initial conversations will provide valuable ideas for adapting the program to meet the particular needs of your congregation.

As you talk with various people and groups, you will discover some who are especially enthusiastic about the prospect of *The Year of the Bible*. Ask them to serve on an ad hoc committee to work out the details of the project. Obviously, it is helpful to approach them with a specific outline of what the committee's activities will involve. A group of six to ten people should be sufficient.

Members of the committee will need to meet approximately once each month prior to the beginning of the year and less frequently once the program is underway. They will engage in the following kinds of tasks:

- Brainstorming ideas to help make the program more effective and to integrate it into as many events in the congregation's life as possible

GETTING GOING: PLANNING FOR THE PROGRAM

- Determining the components of the program as a whole and planning special events
- Helping at specific times when a number of people are needed (for instance, passing out materials, staffing book tables, etc.)
- Praying for the program, both in the planning stages and throughout the year

The committee will be most effective if you seek a variety of types of people to serve on it. All must be enthusiastic about the project, of course. However, you want to be sure that you mix "idea people"—who may or may not be as effective in carrying out the details of the program—with others who have good organizational skills.

For most churches, the decisive step will be seeking formal support for the endeavor from the governing board of the congregation. If you have done your work well, all members of the board will have had a chance to discuss and react to the proposal before you bring it to them officially. Your goal is to secure the full support of the board so that the program can go to the congregation with unanimous endorsement as an official program for your church.

The proposal to the board should make it clear that endorsement by the members of the board involves not only approval of the program, but also a commitment to participate. Otherwise, their endorsement is likely to have a hollow ring to it, and it will not carry much weight with the congregation. Also, the board's approval should involve a commitment from them to help develop *The Year of the Bible* through whatever committees and groups the members of the board work with individually.

Plan to approach the board well in advance of the starting date for the project, preferably in the preceding spring or summer, and certainly by the early fall. You will find on the next page a sample resolution in Figure 1 to use as a guide when you write your proposal.

THE YEAR OF THE BIBLE

A Proposal to [your governing board]

One of the ways people have nourished their faith in Christ is by reading through the entire Bible in a year. While this requires reading fairly large amounts of material on a consistent basis, people who have done it testify to how meaningful it is to them.

I propose that we use this approach as a centerpiece for an entire year's emphasis on the Bible for our congregation. Much more can be done than simply encouraging people to read the Bible daily. We can put together a unified program for the entire year. For instance: the Bible can be the focus for spiritual life, family life, and youth retreats; cantatas in worship can be based on it; sermons can concentrate on the readings for a particular Sunday; and adult seminars can discuss biblical interpretation.

The program, *The Year of the Bible*, by James E. Davison, provides instructions for a comprehensive program that can coordinate all of our activities during the year. Reading the Bible will permeate the entire life of our congregation, and it will have a strong effect on our vitality, commitment, and growth. All of the programs for which our committees are responsible may gain considerably, and there will be benefits for our people in ways that we cannot anticipate in advance.

I recommend that we adopt this program for our congregations for [year]. Adoption means more than simply endorsing the program. For the program to have a vital impact, all of us will need to be involved personally. Specifically, adoption of *The Year of the Bible* will require your commitment to do the following:

1. Participate in the program, by reading the Bible along with the congregation.

2. Support the program, by seeking ways and means to implement it in the life of our congregation (activities and programs of your own committees will be the logical place for this to occur).

I urge you both to commit yourself and to encourage our congregation to dedicate itself to pursuing *The Year of the Bible* in our life together in [year].

FIGURE 1

GETTING GOING: PLANNING FOR THE PROGRAM

DEVELOPING PLANS

For *The Year of the Bible* to operate optimally, you and your committee will need to make decisions about a number of items at an early stage. This will require careful thought and attention to detail, but when the basic planning is in place, much of your work will be done.

As you and the committee formulate the plan, you will probably want to add other components to the points mentioned here. However, the following items cover the primary elements of the program:

1. Develop your logo. Sample B in Appendix 1 offers a design for a logo for *The Year of the Bible*. This is only an example, and you may wish to develop a logo that is individualized for your own congregation. Your logo will be especially attractive if there is a committee member, or someone in the congregation at large, who has professional expertise in design. You will want to be sure to have the logo completed as early as possible because it will appear on all of your materials and publicity items.

2. Make provisions to order the participant's books. Each person ought to have a copy of the participant's book to use as they engage in the program. The book contains the readings from the Bible for each day of the year. Participants can check off the date by each day's readings as a reminder that they have (or have not!) done the readings. In addition, I have supplied a brief discussion of each month's material following the list of daily readings. This material will give a capsule overview of the readings so that people will know what main themes to expect, why some seemingly strange information is included by the biblical writers, and how the passages can be read most effectively and profitably.

The participant's book is the real core of *The Year of the Bible*. It will function not only as a guide to the readings themselves, but it will also serve as a reminder and encouragement to people to keep up with the program. By the end of the year, it will certainly look well worn from regular use by those who complete the readings.

This is a good time to explain how the readings themselves are structured for *The Year of the Bible*. You will notice that participants read approximately two chapters of the Old Testament each day. A third chapter usually comes from the New Testament. Twice each week the New Testament is replaced by one or more psalms. This pattern enables people to read through the Old Testament more or less in sequence. At the same time, it allows readers to take the psalms on a more casual basis, rather than attempting to read all of them in a brief period of time.

As you can imagine, one of the central elements in making the program work effectively is selecting the sermon themes each Sunday from the readings for the day. This is a major challenge for the person who preaches each Sunday because it limits the possibilities for selection of texts. Fortunately, with three chapters of readings each day, there generally should be a significant number of potential themes available. On some special Sundays that the congregation celebrates, it will probably not be possible to relate the theme to the readings for the day. In any case, whoever normally does the preaching in your congregation ought to be aware that they will need to choose sermon texts from the readings.

3. Develop commitment cards. These should be distributed as widely as possible. The value of the card is that it makes a person's commitment to the project more concrete and serious. By signing the card, a person pledges, in a semi-public way, to participate. A sample commitment card is shown in Figure 2 below.

| YOUR LOGO HERE | I plan to participate with the congregation of _____ Church in our special program, *The Year of the Bible*. I will try to read through the entire Bible during the year of _____. |

Name(s) _____ Phone _____
Address _____
_____

FIGURE 2

GETTING GOING: PLANNING FOR THE PROGRAM

4. Create a banner. Placing a banner in the front of the sanctuary will give visual impact to the program. It is an extremely valuable way to keep the program before the congregation. For the banner to be most appealing, enlist someone who is good at creating banners. A special design can be developed for it, or the banner can simply display the logo itself.

5. Create posters. All posters should exhibit the logo. They are intended to help publicize the project, and you can place them in a number of locations throughout the church.

6. Plan a resource table. Look for a space in a well-travelled location in the church where you can set up a table for the duration of the program. Determine what will be placed on the table and who will be responsible for maintaining the displays. The resource table can be used for a number of purposes. Here are examples of some things you can do:

- Establish a box in which people can deposit questions about the readings.
- Maintain a library display, updating it each month.
- Install a bulletin board where someone on the committee can display cartoons and newspaper articles on biblical topics relevant to the readings.
- Exhibit articles from the Holy Land, if such are available to you.
- Set up maps and pictures related to the readings.

7. Recommend Bible versions. One of the questions people ask most frequently as they prepare to begin this project is what translation of the Bible they should use. In an effort to provide guidance, place an article on this subject on your resource table in December. Run the same article in your January newsletter. You can use Sample C in Appendix 1 as a guide in composing an article with advice on the topic.

8. Encourage committees to begin planning. Most committees and groups should already have been notified of the plans. Now it is important to approach them again, this time asking them to begin drafting specific plans for incorporating their programs into the overall scheme of *The Year of the Bible*.

This is especially critical in cases where a committee plans far in advance. This may be the case with those who are organizing a churchwide retreat for the congregation or for those who are sketching out the themes for youth retreats.

9. Explore options with adult church school classes. If possible, you should use *The Year of the Bible* as the theme for the classes throughout the year. This will give people the opportunity to engage in discussion of the passages they are reading. Depending on the structure of your church school for adults, it may or may not be feasible to focus all educational efforts on this program. However, if all classes do participate, it will have a particularly powerful effect in unifying the life of the congregation's church school program.

You should be aware that there is one potential problem with this idea. Lay teachers may express discomfort about having to prepare lessons without the benefit of a teacher's guide, which usually comes with curricular materials. Those concerns can be addressed by providing them with teaching materials. You may wish to develop these resources yourself, or you can probably find sufficient helps for the leaders from a curriculum that your church has used in the past.

Another possibility is to design a Bible study that prepares the leaders to lead their classes. This will require more time and energy, of course, but it could be an excellent opportunity for a year-long period of teacher/leader training.

10. Consider possibilities for small group ministries. In some congregations, small groups are a large part of the life of the church. Other congregations have only a few, if any, such groups in operation. The structure varies from congregation to congregation, but the primary elements usually focus on a combination of fellowship, prayer, and Bible study. To integrate small groups in your congregation into *The Year of the Bible* will require special planning since the schedule for these groups, which likely meet once every week or two, will probably not match the outline of readings in the program.

The easiest approach here is to confirm the schedule of meeting dates for these groups. Then choose one chapter from the readings for the previous

GETTING GOING: PLANNING FOR THE PROGRAM

six days as the material for the Bible study portion for each of the meeting dates. Try to coordinate the chapters you choose around a central theme in order to give more continuity to the study. For instance, if a group meets from February 21 to April 3, you could select passages from Acts and Romans and use Paul's ministry and message as an overarching theme for the series of studies. See Figure 3 below for an example.

PAUL: HIS MINISTRY AND MESSAGE		
Week	*Passage*	*Topic*
Feb. 14–20	———	Introduction
Feb. 21–27	Acts 9	Paul's Conversion
Feb. 28–Mar. 6	Acts 13	The First Journey Begins
Mar. 7–13	Acts 17	Paul at Athens
Mar. 14–20	Acts 20	Eutychus and Ephesus
Mar. 21–27	Acts 28	From Malta to Rome

FIGURE 3

Again, you may need to give special attention to the leaders in order to be certain that they are comfortable with their own understanding of the passages that their groups will be discussing.

11. Plan options for children in your church school. Naturally, you will not want to have children do all the readings from *The Year of the Bible* since many adults will have trouble with that! You can easily do special projects through the church school, and you can continually stress the project to the children. Ask the leaders of your church school to concentrate their efforts on this program for the year. With a little encouragement, they will likely find a host of ways to weave the theme of the Bible into their plans. By the way, be sure to recommend to parents, too, that they read some of the material with their children from a version of the Bible that is specifically aimed at children. There are many of these available in local denominational and nondenominational bookstores.

PROJECTING YOUR COSTS

"What will it cost?" is a question that you may hear early on. In spite of the complexity of the program, you may be surprised to learn that the expenses associated with it are not at all high. Here are the significant items to keep in mind as you estimate your costs.

1. Procuring participant's books. As I mentioned above, the book is the nucleus for the entire *The Year of the Bible* program. Those who take part will be using it virtually every day all year long. Since it is reasonable to ask those who participate to buy their own book, this should not be a major cost for your budget. There will be some expense in procuring copies of the book in the first place, but most of that outlay will filter back to your budget as people pick up their copies.

That said, I recommend that you estimate generously the number of copies you will need. Be sure to order them early too. There are two primary reasons for this. In the first place, the book will serve as a publicity piece to help attract people to sign up for the program. Displaying it in a convenient, highly traveled area in your building will help convince people to participate. In the second place, those who do sign up will want copies in their hands to get a feel for the program. In fact, some will want to start reading in advance.

Once the year is underway, you should continue to make copies available in the church. Throughout the first few months of the program, people are likely to pick up additional copies for a variety of reasons. They may decide to join the program themselves, or they may want to secure copies for friends and relatives.

2. Printing commitment cards. While these cards should look attractive, they do not need to be professionally printed. You can set up your own design according to the suggestions earlier. Most copiers these days will reproduce masters on cardstock. That is a sufficient weight paper to give some substance to the cards (and the commitment they indicate!). Plan on cards that are 4.25" by 5.5" in size. Then you can produce four cards at a time through a copier. In this way, the expense involved ought to be minimal.

GETTING GOING: PLANNING FOR THE PROGRAM

3. Printing certificates of achievement. Since you will have an accurate count of participants in the program, you will be able to make a reliable estimate of the cost of certificates. For budgetary purposes, keep in mind that the certificates do not need to be printed until near the end of the year.

4. Copying materials. If you have a copier in the church office, you can produce many of your materials in-house. These costs can be absorbed into your church's regular office expenses because they will undoubtedly be only a fraction of your overall congregational budget.

5. Implementing special events. Depending on how many and what kind of additional events you hold, you should assume that you will encounter a few miscellaneous expenses during the year. For example, you may want to provide light snacks for an end-of-the-year party. Another minor cost will be the materials for your banner.

6. Providing additional library resources. If you have a librarian in your church, that person may wish to update the library's holdings to include additional materials relevant to the program. Lay-oriented commentaries as well as books illustrating biblical life and times are examples. Consider procuring a set of audiotapes of the Bible too. The library budget may be able to cover these costs. Otherwise, you can include them in your own estimates for the program.

If you do have someone who serves as the librarian for the congregation, you have some good news for that person. He or she will undoubtedly be happy to know that one of the certain spin-offs of *The Year of the Bible* program is that use of the library will increase significantly.

Naturally, the earlier you are able to accomplish all of the tasks outlined in this chapter, the more smoothly organizing and implementing *The Year of the Bible* will proceed. Chapter 2 will take up the next steps: publicizing the program and initiating the year itself within your congregation.

CHAPTER 2
STARTING UP: INAUGURATING THE YEAR

PUBLICIZING THE PROGRAM

Publicity is an extremely important element in generating the enthusiasm and excitement necessary to make *The Year of the Bible* a successful venture for your congregation. There are many possibilities to consider as you plan your publicity. Your strategy will undoubtedly vary somewhat from this listing, but here are the primary areas that need to be considered.

1. Initial announcement to the congregation. The congregation should hear well in advance about the beginning of *The Year of the Bible* program and should be aware that you will be calling for their commitment to participate. This gives them the chance to become familiar with the idea before being asked specifically to participate. Choose a Sunday in the fall (October is not too early) as the date to announce the plans publicly.

Consider making the Bible the theme of the service and use the occasion to present your plans and your hopes for congregational involvement.

2. Advance written publicity. A church newsletter is the principal means of communication in many congregations. In conjunction with your initial announcement to the congregation, include articles about the program in your church's newsletter. You will want to outline the value of reading the Bible and the plans for the year.

Publish these articles with the logo attached. If your congregation does not publish a newsletter, you may want to send this communication in the form of a personal letter. Appendix 1 contains materials for an article in the early fall (Sample D) and for one that can be printed as a follow-up piece (Sample E). It will prove worthwhile to develop some light-hearted publicity pieces to interest people in this project. An example of such an article, based on the idea of "top ten reasons," is also contained in Appendix 1 (Sample F).

3. Bulletin announcements. During the sign-up period in December, you will want to place announcements in the Sunday bulletins. These announcements can be brief, but they should also be direct. Ask people to commit themselves to this major adventure in your congregational life together. Figure 1 on the next page contains some examples of possible announcements.

SAMPLE BULLETIN ANNOUNCEMENTS

First Sunday in December

Sign-ups are underway for *The Year of the Bible*. By now you should have received a commitment card with your December newsletter, which gives details of our plans. This program will be the focus of the entire coming year. Please turn in your commitment card to the church office and pick up a copy of the participant's book that goes with the program.

Second Sunday in December

Plan now to have a blessed New Year! Join us in *The Year of the Bible* program for [year]. Here's your chance to grow spiritually in the coming year. You will need to set aside about twenty minutes a day to participate in your joint program. Many members have already indicated that they will be doing the readings. Please return your commitment card so we will know how many people are joining in this endeavor.

Third Sunday in December

If you don't have your card in for *The Year of the Bible*, please send it in as soon as possible. We are looking forward to a great year and many of our congregation have already said that they plan to be a part of the program. Don't miss out!

FIGURE 1

4. *Bulletin insert*. Place an insert in your bulletin on the first Sunday of registration for the program. Additional copies can be placed in literature racks and other locations around the church. Samples G and H in Appendix 1 contain material for a two-sided insert for your bulletin.

5. *Local newspapers*. Since this is a unique program, your local papers may consider it newsworthy. Send a brief announcement to the newspapers in your area. Better yet, call your local newspapers. Encourage the person who is responsible for religious news to write a feature article on the program. If you submit your own written material, you can pattern it after the example in Figure 2 below.

ARTICLE FOR LOCAL NEWSPAPER

The Bible will be the theme for the entire year of [year] at [name of church]. The congregation has accepted a challenge to read through the whole Bible in one year. A book will guide participants as they read approximately twenty minutes a day.

With the readings as the focus for the year, the congregation will be concentrating on the Scriptures in all of its programming. Retreats, special music in worship, and many other programs will have the Bible as their theme. It is expected that all who participate in the readings will find the year stimulating, their faith strengthened, and their lives richer.

For further information, contact the church office [phone number].

FIGURE 2

INSTITUTING THE YEAR

The invitation to sign up for *The Year of the Bible* will need to be a concerted effort involving you and the committee. In addition to the materials you provide explaining plans for the year, the enthusiasm all of you display for the project will convince members of the congregation to participate.

STARTING UP: INAUGURATING THE YEAR

Plan the major push for the entire month of December. Encourage people to sign cards as early as possible, but be prepared to continue receiving commitment cards well into January. You should assume that, for a variety of reasons, it may be early February before you have a complete list of those who are participating. Even then, your list of participants will probably not be absolutely complete.

Well into the year there will probably be people in your congregation who, for one reason or another, chose not to join the program when it was first announced, but who now wish they had become part of it. Their own schedules may have changed, allowing them to take the time necessary to do the readings. Perhaps they have simply become more excited about the project because they see others involved in it. For the first few months of the year, therefore, you should continue to suggest that it is not too late to join the program. Offering occasional, brief invitations to join *The Year of the Bible* may bring additional people into the program. Figures 3 and 4 on the following page offer sample articles that may be of help.

In summary, here is an outline of the basic steps you will follow as you institute *The Year of the Bible*:

1. About the beginning of November, circulate commitment cards to members of the church board and committees. Your goal is to have as many people as possible already signed up before the program is presented to the congregation. This will serve as an encouragement for the rest of the congregation to join too.

2. At the beginning of December, send letters of invitation and commitment cards to each household in your congregation. These can be attached to the church newsletter if you send one to members.

3. On the first Sunday of December, run an insert in the bulletin that encourages people to sign cards and to prepare for the coming year.

4. On each Sunday in December, include an announcement in the bulletin reminding people to join.

5. During some or all of your services in December, have different members of the congregation give brief "minutes for mission" or

> ### WANT TO JOIN *THE YEAR OF THE BIBLE*?
>
> Even if you were not able to start last month when our special *The Year of the Bible* program got underway, it's not too late to join. There are three easy steps:
>
> 1. Pick up a participant's book.
> 2. Fill in a commitment card and return it to the church office.
> 3. Start reading!
>
> Start where the group is now. Then over the next month or so, try to catch up with the earlier readings in Genesis and Matthew. Before long, you'll be completely up to date.

FIGURE 3

> ### WISH YOU HAD STARTED? START NOW!
>
> It's still not too late to get into our *The Year of the Bible* program. If you couldn't start in January, or if you have found that you have more time available than you had expected, or if the project sounds more intriguing than it did then, join now!
>
> You can start in [month] and read until [month] of next year, using a full twelve months. Or (if you are really courageous!) you might try to catch up on the earlier readings and finish with the rest of us at the end of December.
>
> Either way, read the [month] through December materials along with the group. You will get more enjoyment by being in the same section of the Scriptures that the rest of us are reading.

FIGURE 4

STARTING UP: INAUGURATING THE YEAR

"testimonials" about their hopes for the coming year.

6. In as many sermons in December as possible, emphasize the importance and value of full congregational participation in *The Year of the Bible*.

7. Set up the resource table for the entire month of December. Arrange to have committee members at the table each Sunday to answer questions and encourage participation. Copies of the brochure, commitment cards, and other materials should be available on the table.

8. Organize a dedication service for Sunday morning worship on the first Sunday of January. If the first Sunday happens to fall near January 1 and you expect the attendance to be rather low, you may want to wait for the second Sunday. If the congregation follows the liturgical calendar, Epiphany Sunday is a convenient—and appropriate—Sunday to choose.

This last step deserves a little more elaboration because it can do much to establish the significance of the entire *The Year of the Bible* program in people's minds. The theme for the worship service can be the Bible. Set aside a portion of the service when people who have signed up are asked to stand. A few words of dedication and a prayer for sustenance and strength are appropriate. The joy of this event is heightened when people look around and see a large portion of the congregation standing.

The dedication service is the final event in instituting *The Year of the Bible*. It should be as festive and encouraging as possible. Focus on the program in as many ways as you can. For instance, you can print the logo on the cover of the bulletin for that Sunday. (In fact, you may want to print the logo on the bulletin cover every Sunday for the duration of the program.) Another possibility is to place a second insert about the project in the bulletin itself. The goal is to provide a worship service that will inspire and motivate people as they begin their readings so that they embark on this year-long journey with a sense that the church supports them and the Spirit undergirds them for their task.

CHAPTER 3
THE LONG HAUL: MAINTAINING ENTHUSIASM

*O*nce *The Year of the Bible* is underway, most of the planning will be done. Now, however, you will need to concentrate on maintaining the enthusiasm that people felt initially because it will not be long before some participants discover that it is difficult to keep up with their readings.

The committee should continue to meet occasionally. Since most of the planning has been done, committee members can focus on looking for trouble spots and making sure that the program continues to run smoothly. Ask them to think of ways to connect *The Year of the Bible* to other events and activities in the life of the congregation.

I cannot stress too frequently that what determines how effectively *The Year of the Bible* program will work is the degree to which it is integrated into the whole life of the congregation. The opportunities to do so are almost limitless. In fact, you will discover that it is impossible to envision in advance all the potential ways that the program can be linked with other activities in your congregational life. Thus, I cannot emphasize enough the importance of having the committee brainstorm ideas not only in the planning stages, but also as the year progresses.

REGULAR FEATURES

The real challenge for the leadership of this program is to sustain the interest of those who have made the commitment to participate. The primary method to accomplish this is highlighting *The Year of the Bible* continuously through a number of elements that will recur on a week-to-week basis. Some of these will have to be developed as the year progresses. For instance:

- Sermon preparation using the texts for the day (or the preceding week)
- Teaching Bible classes from the readings for the week
- Maintenance of the displays on the Bible table

Although it is possible to do some advance planning for each of these elements, you cannot avoid regular preparation or supervision as the year progresses.

Fortunately, the two most central features of the program do not need to be developed through the course of the year. Both the participant's book and the weekly questions and answers for the bulletin will be ready to go when the year commences. We need to look at each of these elements of the program in more detail.

1. The participant's book. This book is really the centerpiece of *The Year of the Bible* program. Not only does it contain the readings for each day of the year, but it also includes an overview article for each month's readings. More than anything else, it is possession and use of this book that will get participants through the entire Bible successfully. As mentioned previously,

THE LONG HAUL: MAINTAINING ENTHUSIASM

the daily readings for *The Year of the Bible* alternate between Old and New Testaments. This injects some much-needed variation into the readings and keeps people from feeling that they are mired in the Old Testament for weeks or months on end.

Still, you should bear in mind that there are drawbacks to this arrangement. The very movement from Old Testament to New Testament, and then back again, can be confusing. This problem is intensified by the fact that the biblical readings come from many different authors, living in quite different times. Consequently, the underlying unity of the Scriptures is not always apparent. Add to this the fact that most people do not know much about the cultures of the ancient world, and the likelihood of confusion increases rapidly.

In the best of all possible worlds, everyone participating in *The Year of the Bible* would read a commentary, or at least consult the footnotes in a good study Bible, as they read the material from the Bible. Since you cannot expect most people to do this, it is vital to offer people some alternative other than studying in detail or doing no extra reading at all. That is the purpose of the articles in the participant's book.

The monthly articles suggest to participants what they should look for as they read the Bible and what the primary themes of the passages are. In a brief review of the readings, it is impossible to touch on all of the themes or, depending on the month, all of the books that are to be read. At least it is possible, however, to provide a thread that will help people weave their way through the material.

One further note on the articles in the participant's book: I have tried to avoid discussing controversial matters in theology and biblical interpretation. Nevertheless, the wisdom of the old rabbinic adage is true in Christian circles as well: Where there are three rabbis, there are four opinions.

We all look at things differently, and our interpretations are not always the same. Thus, I encourage you to provide additional material to the participants occasionally, possibly in the newsletter or in the form of handouts available on the resource table.

As I mentioned earlier, each participant who signs up for the program will need a copy of the participant's book. Have extra copies on display in a prominent location. This will help to keep *The Year of the Bible* program before the eyes of the whole congregation, and it may draw additional people into the program as the year goes along.

2. *Weekly questions and answers.* Each week, place in the worship bulletin two or three questions related to the coming week's readings. Each bulletin should also contain the answers to the previous week's questions. The primary purpose of the questions is to give people something to look for as they read. To highlight the questions more fully, you can place them in a box in the bulletin. An obvious location for the answers to the previous week's questions is just prior to the questions for the upcoming week. If you adopt this procedure, the questions and answers will look something like the sample shown in Figure 1. All of this material can be collected with the announcements for that week, or you can find another appropriate location elsewhere in the bulletin.

In Appendix 2, you will find a list of questions and answers to draw

---

ANSWERS TO *THE YEAR OF THE BIBLE*: WEEK 16

Judges tells us about 700 left-handers who could hit a hair with a sling (Judg. 20:16); Ruth's great-grandson is David, the king of Israel (Ruth 4:17–22); At the transfiguration, Moses and Elijah appear with Jesus (Mark 9:4).

THE YEAR OF THE BIBLE: WEEK 17

1 Samuel 4—19; Psalms 46—48; Mark 10—14

How does Saul show mercy shortly after becoming king?

Why does Saul become angry with David?

From what book and chapter does Jesus quote when he is asked which commandment is greatest?

FIGURE 1

THE LONG HAUL: MAINTAINING ENTHUSIASM

from as you prepare the bulletin material. Enough questions have been included so that you will not need to write many questions each week. Because each year begins on a different day, the readings for any given week will vary depending on the year in which the program is being used. Consequently, questions and answers are listed according to the day and month to which each question applies. If you offer two questions per week, choose one from the Old Testament and one from the New Testament. If you provide three questions each week, I recommend that you choose two questions from the Old Testament and one from the New Testament.

You will discover that developing good questions is a difficult but enjoyable task. Keep the following principles in mind when writing questions:

- Write questions that are clear, concise, and straightforward.
- Write questions that are easy for people to find answers for as they read.
- Write questions that embody a specific point with some teaching value (that is, questions that are more than "trivia").

You will find that it is not always easy to develop questions that fit all these criteria. In particular, the third principle is difficult to apply consistently, given the need to keep the questions clear and concise.

ADDITIONAL POSSIBILITIES

While these regular features are the primary means to enhance *The Year of the Bible*, you will want to consider other possibilities as well. Here are additional ideas to incorporate into the program on a regular or occasional basis.

1. Brief articles in the church newsletter. There are many possibilities here. Invite some of the members of the congregation to contribute articles. First-person accounts by lay members are especially interesting to people. You can run pieces that deal with individuals' experiences related to the readings, offer encouragement to others, and suggest ideas for reading more efficiently.

You can also include a variety of other articles in the newsletter. An article for parents on choosing a children's Bible is one possibility. Since people sometimes seem uncertain about what the structural plan of the readings really is, a brief article, such as the one in Figure 2, may be helpful.

In February or March, an article encouraging people who have fallen behind may also be of use. There is a sample of such an article in Appendix 1, Sample I. The committee will be able to develop a number of other ideas as well.

THE READING SCHEDULE

Some people have asked if there is any special plan behind the set of readings we are using for *The Year of the Bible*. There is, but it is simple. The approach is designed primarily to keep us from reading all of the Old Testament straight through. It tends to be more difficult (and less familiar) for people than the New Testament. In this schedule of readings, the Old and New Testaments are interspersed. Also, the psalms are spread throughout the year, which is an easier way to read them.

FIGURE 2

Now and then, print in the newsletter a few especially significant quotations from the materials read the previous month. Ask people to submit Scripture quotations that were especially meaningful to them. You can also ask someone on the committee to look for a few quotations each month as they read along. These quotations can then be published in the next month's newsletter. At the end of the year, you might even print all of the quotations and distribute them with the end-of-the-year materials under the title "Our Favorite Scripture Quotations."

2. A question box on the resource table. As people read sections of the Bible that they have not read in a long time, if ever, they will be surprised at what they find. In some cases, *shock* may be the more accurate term for their reactions. Consider placing a question box (with paper and pencils) on the

THE LONG HAUL: MAINTAINING ENTHUSIASM

resource table. Answers to questions received can be posted on a bulletin board on or near the table. Alternatively, some of these questions and answers can be published in the newsletter.

You will probably discover that people will submit questions regularly during the early part of the year, but that gradually fewer and fewer questions will appear. This is a natural result as *The Year of the Bible* becomes more routine and as some of the initial enthusiasm diminishes. Including a reminder in the newsletter, such as the one in Sample I, in Appendix 1, may prompt more questions.

Generally speaking, it is essential to provide answers to the questions you receive in a timely fashion. Now and then, however, more questions may be submitted than you can possibly handle within a reasonable time period. If you set up a question box, therefore, you should make it clear that you may not always be able to provide an answer as promptly as you would like.

Most of the questions that people submit will be interesting. Whereas in some cases the answer may be straightforward, in others a response will not come easily. Some examples of the kinds of questions you may expect to receive during the year are included in Figure 3 on the next page.

QUESTIONS READERS ASK

"My version of the Bible says that Jacob makes Joseph a long robe with sleeves. Where and why did the 'coat of many colors' appear? (Gen. 37:3)?"

"In the records of descendants in the Old Testament, why aren't women mentioned?"

"What were 'blemishes' that would disqualify a bull (or other animal) from being used as a sin offering? (Lev. 9:2)"

"Things keep getting bloodier! In 1 Samuel 15:33, 'Samuel hewed Agag in pieces before the Lord in Gilgal.' Why that phrase 'before the Lord' in regard to this violent act? Does it suggest the Lord's enjoyment or approval? Did these people not believe that every act they performed was 'before the Lord'?"

"Matthew traces the genealogy of Christ through Joseph. How does that square with the virgin birth?"

"Why were Paul and Timothy forbidden by the Holy Spirit to speak the Word in Asia? (Acts 16:6)"

FIGURE 3

As you can see, answering the questions may be taxing at times. It is fair to admit in your response to a given question that you do not have a good answer. With some particularly complex or vexing questions that have no clear-cut solutions, you may simply want to indicate various possible answers.

3. Special Sunday emphases. Periodically throughout the year, stress *The Year of the Bible* as a special theme in Sunday morning services. When and how you do this will depend on the structure of the church calendar. If there is a "Bible Sunday" on the calendar of events, this is an opportune time to highlight the program. Other possibilities are to link this emphasis to the

THE LONG HAUL: MAINTAINING ENTHUSIASM

major Sundays of the liturgical calendar or to plan a special event every two months or once per quarter.

Consider having a special service to celebrate the half-way point of the program. It is effective to have people involved in the endeavor lead the service. Instead of the usual Sunday morning sermon, for instance, consider inviting two or three people to speak for five minutes each on the meaning of the program for them.

Special celebrations provide the opportunity to encourage people to keep up—or to catch up if they are behind. Early in the year, such special Sundays are excellent times to invite people who are not part of the program to join. As mentioned previously, new readers should begin where the group as a whole is reading; otherwise, they will not feel part of the overall program. The most obvious discrepancy is that new participants would not be reading the passages that are the basis for the Sunday sermons.

4. Letters to participants. A few times during the year it is helpful to correspond directly with everyone in the program. Another option is to call people individually. Depending on the number of people participating, you and the committee may be able to do this once or twice during the year.

The primary purpose of either means of communication is simply to provide you with another way to encourage people to continue their readings. The letters can be used for other purposes too: to highlight upcoming events, to encourage people to join a church school class, and to ask people to suggest additional ideas for the program.

When writing to participants in the middle of the summer, you may want to enclose a survey card asking them to let you know how they are doing. Since the response rate to surveys is generally not very good, only a minority of cards will probably be returned, but those that do come back can be encouraging! You may receive comments like these:

"I've found this experience to be both challenging and inspirational. I'm glad I made this commitment."

"I read first thing in the morning as I sip my cup of coffee. I look forward to that quiet time each day."

"The discipline of reading the Bible is helping me to adhere to other schedules that I need to follow."

Someone may even respond with a comment like this: "Are you sure the *Reader's Digest* version of the Old Testament wouldn't have been a brilliant translation to use?"

Figure 4 illustrates a survey card that can be sent to your members.

MID-YEAR SURVEY CARD

How are you doing in your readings at the moment?
Please check one:

"Believe it or not, I am................Ahead of Schedule."_____
"I'm proud (relieved?) to say, I am ....Up to Date."_____
"Thank goodness I am ....Nearly on Schedule."_____
"Woe is me, I am ....Pretty Far Behind."_____

Comments and suggestions:

_____   _____
(Date)   Name (optional)

FIGURE 4

The possibilities for integrating various aspects of congregational life into one, all-encompassing *The Year of the Bible* program are almost inexhaustible. You cannot do everything, and at a certain point you will likely have to omit some ideas and possibilities simply because of lack of time and energy. However, you and the committee must be sure that the primary elements of the program continue constantly and effectively. As participants see that the church is committed to *The Year of the Bible* not only in January

THE LONG HAUL: MAINTAINING ENTHUSIASM

and February, but also in June and July and in October and November, they will be encouraged to keep up with the readings themselves.

Let me offer two final words of advice. First, bear in mind that not everyone who begins the program will be able to keep up for the entire year. Some will find their business and travel schedules too demanding; others may fall too far behind because of illness, changes in their work, or a death in the family. Still others may not be able to organize their lives in such a way that they can manage the readings day in and day out. In order to avoid the danger of persons in these sorts of situations harboring guilt feelings, make it clear at various times and in various ways that you are aware of the kinds of extenuating circumstances that may keep persons from completing the program.

Second, be sure to update the governing board regularly about the progress of the endeavor. Since their approval was given for *The Year of the Bible* program, it is only proper that you keep them informed. Moreover, as the official leadership of the congregation, their continuing enthusiasm for the project will aid greatly in keeping up the momentum as the months pass.

CHAPTER 4
WRAPPING UP: CONCLUDING THE PROGRAM

The end of the year, like the beginning, requires careful preparation. Broadly speaking, you will need to proceed in two directions: (1) closing activities and (2) follow-up plans. This chapter suggests a number of possibilities for you to consider in both of these categories.

CLOSING ACTIVITIES

When the congregation finishes *The Year of the Bible*, it will have accomplished an uncommon feat. The achievement should be celebrated! Here are a number of suggestions for end-of-the-year events. As you and the committee plan, think of other possibilities too.

   1. Certificates of participation. Some sort of visible token of participation in *The Year of the Bible* is a necessity. The program is unique, and it constitutes a major challenge. Those who have completed the readings should receive something concrete to remember the achievement.

Although all sorts of awards are available, either through mail-order catalogs or church supply companies, I recommend that you present certificates of recognition as mementos of this program. Certificates are particularly appropriate awards for completing *The Year of the Bible*. Not only can you print the logo on the certificates, but you can also make certificates a size that allows participants to place them in their Bibles. A sample certificate is shown in Figure 1.

YOUR LOGO HERE

"The Lord has done great things for us."
(Psalm 126:3)

THE YEAR OF THE BIBLE

Presented to _____
in recognition of your participation in reading through the Bible
in _____.

_____
(signed)

FIGURE 1

Of course, you will need to consider costs when determining the design and printing specifications for the certificates. Designing personalized certificates will be significantly less expensive than purchasing ready-made awards. A printer can lay out and print the design on quality paper at a reasonable cost. This cost can be further reduced if one of the church members has a personal computer with a good graphics software package. He or she will be able to create an attractive, professional-looking certificate. In this case, the costs will be limited to the number of certificates printed.

WRAPPING UP: CONCLUDING THE PROGRAM

Ask a member of the congregation who writes with a fine hand to print each person's name on a certificate. To give the certificate a more personal touch, have each one signed individually by the person or persons most involved in the planning of the program. The additional time it takes to sign the certificates is well worth the effort.

Another decision that you and the committee must make in advance is how to plan to distribute the certificates. The most convenient method is to give them out to people in conjunction with other closing activities, such as a service of recognition or an end-of-the-year party. Since not everyone will attend these activities, you will need to contact some people to arrange to get their certificates to them.

It is possible that some members who did not sign up for the program will have been reading along with the congregation. In order to find out who they are, print a note in the bulletin or newsletter suggesting that they let someone know that they have completed the readings. Figure 2 offers a sample note to consider.

A SPECIAL NOTE TO "SECRET" READERS

To those of you who may have been participating in *The Year of the Bible*, but never signed a card: Please let the church office know of your involvement. We would like to know how many people have been reading and, if you have finished, we want to give you a certificate as a memento of the year.

FIGURE 2

There is also another issue to consider. Not everyone who sets out to read the entire Bible in one year will make it through all of the readings. If people simply give up at some point during the year, they should not receive certificates. Still, what do you do with those who cannot finish during the year but wish to keep reading until they do complete the readings? I recommend that these people let someone know when they have finished so that they can be issued a certificate at that time.

My reasoning here is this: Since the ultimate goal of the program is to encourage people to read the Scriptures, the fact that people actually finish reading the whole Bible is more important than whether or not they are able to complete the readings within the one-year time period. A note I received several months after the end of the first *The Year of the Bible* program is indicative of the kind of thing you may hear:

"I have finally completed reading the Bible in its entirety. Maybe I should have called it, 'The Year and a Half of the Bible.' Thanks for the opportunity to accomplish something I've thought many times about. Now I can at long last say, 'I've read THE BOOK from cover to cover.'"

This kind of comment convinces me that this is the best way to deal with people who are unable to finish their readings within a twelve-month period. It allows for a way to encourage those who are having difficulty keeping up with the schedule to continue reading.

2. Service of recognition. I suggested earlier that the congregation consider having a dedication service to inaugurate *The Year of the Bible*. It is fitting to close the year formally in a similar fashion. You may choose to set the service of recognition one year later on the same Sunday that you held the dedication service. It will be exciting, exactly one year later, to think back to the beginnings and realize what you have accomplished since then.

The actual recognition of participants may be one particular segment within the service as a whole. You may or may not attempt to orient the whole service around the theme of *The Year of the Bible*. It is easy to do this, however, and you should consider this approach as you plan. Regardless of which option is selected, the more important concern is what is said during

WRAPPING UP: CONCLUDING THE PROGRAM

the service of recognition.

The comments can focus on two particular thoughts. As you might guess, the first is the value of the Scriptures as the Word of God. A number of verses from Psalm 119 provide excellent quotations for this purpose. (However, I do not recommend quoting the whole of Psalm 119!) The second thought is gratitude. Thank people for participating, and, more important, express your gratitude to God for the guidance, strength, and grace that made the program possible.

3. End-of-the-year party. In conjunction with the service of recognition, you may want to organize a party. This celebration could follow immediately upon the service itself. For instance, you might adjourn to the fellowship hall for a "pot-luck" dinner. An alternative is to hold a completely separate event, perhaps an early evening gathering with light refreshments.

Give people the opportunity to share some of their reactions to what they have read. Questions such as "What did you find most surprising?" and "What was most interesting to you?" are useful for this purpose. Add to the fun by dividing into teams to play a Bible quiz game. As the final event of the evening, I suggest that Revelation 22 be read in unison. It is especially satisfying to finish the program officially by reading together the last chapter of the New Testament. Regardless of the type of event, be sure to publicize it widely. See Figure 3 for an example.

LET'S CELEBRATE!

You are invited (whether you are part of *The Year of the Bible* program or not) to come to church on [date] for a brief celebration. *All ages are welcome.* We'll have some games and refreshments, and to cap off our readings, we'll read the last chapter of the book of Revelation together.

FIGURE 3

In the publicity, make clear whether or not children are invited. If you do want children to be present, plan a party that allows for their full participation. There is considerable merit in having children witness the value that the congregation has placed on reading the Bible.

4. Summary article in church newsletter. In January of the calendar year following *The Year of the Bible*, write a brief summary of the program along with a word of thanks not only to everyone who participated, but also to all who helped during the year. You can include a few words from the comments of some of the people who participated. Figure J in Appendix 1 contains a sample of an article to run in your church newsletter.

A variation of this article could concentrate on testimonials of people who participated in the program. Pick three or four people for whom the year has been an especially compelling experience and interview them or ask them to write about their reactions. Include their comments in the newsletter along with their photographs. This will add visual appeal to the articles and help to personalize even more your summary of the program. You can then limit your own article to a very brief statement of thanks to all who were involved.

FOLLOW-UP PLANS

As important as *The Year of the Bible* is, it is not an end in itself. The ultimate purpose of the program is to acquaint people with the Scriptures and to encourage them to read the Bible regularly after the program has ended. Much of the effect of this effort will be unmeasurable, of course. It is difficult to quantify categories such as "appreciation" and "enthusiasm." You can be assured, however, that many participants will be sufficiently motivated by their readings that they will want to continue with some sort of specific format for future Bible study.

In fact, toward the end of the year, people will probably mention a desire to continue reading the Bible in some form or other during the following year. This is one of the best indicators that the program has been

WRAPPING UP: CONCLUDING THE PROGRAM

successful! Let's look at some of the kinds of things that you can do to build on the interest in Bible study that has grown through the year.

1. Make other programs of readings available. You may already have on hand another plan for reading the Scriptures on a regular basis. As *The Year of the Bible* draws to a close, inform participants that this plan will be made available to them. You may want to look for other programs as well. Consult with church educators in nearby congregations, visit a denominational bookstore, or browse through publishers' catalogs. With a little effort, you will undoubtedly turn up a wide range of possibilities.

2. Make available additional copies of the participant's book. As the year draws to a close, you will discover that some people will want to utilize the schedule of readings again, either immediately or in the future. Others, who were unable to participate the first time around, may want to begin reading during the following year. The beauty of the reading schedule is that it can be used any year. Thus, it is worthwhile to keep a supply of the participant's books available for the congregation. They will continue to disappear from the literature rack, sometimes to be used by the purchaser and sometimes to be sent to a friend or relative as a present.

3. Offer a new program for the following year. The suggestions mentioned above assume that you will provide a range of possible programs for people to utilize individually in the ensuing year, or years. An alternative is to develop and conduct a new program as a follow-up project for the next year. You can adopt a similar scheme to the one used for *The Year of the Bible*. For instance, you can write monthly overview articles for the church newsletter, and you can continue to place a few questions about upcoming readings in the weekly bulletins. You can develop a logo to go along with the program as well.

This follow-up effort probably should not be a congregation-wide undertaking. Publicize it broadly, but present it as simply a systematic method for those who wish to continue reading the Scriptures with other people in a guided program. In this manner, you can extend the enthusiasm initiated by *The Year of the Bible* into the next year without putting pressure on those people—probably the majority of your readers—who need a respite from the readings and are not yet ready to take on another project like this.

I encourage you to provide some specific follow-up program. Interest in continued reading of the Bible, albeit in a less rigorous fashion, will be strong at this time, and you will not want to miss the chance for further education and spiritual growth among the participants that this opportunity provides.

4. Offer an in-depth Bible course. If you have ever wanted to offer the congregation an intensive Bible study, such as one of the national programs that are available, this is the time to do so! By the end of *The Year of the Bible*, enthusiasm for the Scriptures will be high, and people will express the desire to gain a more profound understanding of the Bible. They will be ripe for serious study of the Scriptures, and you will want to take advantage of the opportunity.

Determine well in advance what particular program will be used. Most of the national programs that are available offer suggestions about such things as scheduling, advertising, and implementation. It is not necessary to repeat those sorts of suggestions here. Suffice it to say that *The Year of the Bible* will create such a positive climate that it may well provide the most favorable opportunity to introduce the congregation to intensive Bible study.

5. Promote existing Bible study groups. Most churches have a variety of Bible study classes. In Chapter 1, I suggested that you seek to implement *The Year of the Bible* as the curriculum for some or all of your adult church school classes. Participation in *The Year of the Bible*, therefore, may already have effected an increased enrollment in some of your church school classes. Still, at the end of the year, you will probably encounter people who have not yet become active in one of these classes, but who now voice a desire to continue studying the Scriptures. This is your opportunity to invite them to join a Sunday morning church school class!

The congregation probably offers Bible studies not only on Sunday mornings, but at other times of the week as well. There may be other kinds of groups for fellowship, faith sharing, and spiritual growth, in which Bible

WRAPPING UP: CONCLUDING THE PROGRAM

study is a significant component. These, too, provide good occasions for gaining greater knowledge of the Bible. Advertise all of these opportunities to members and encourage them to join the one that appears to best fit their needs and interests.

The goal of all of these suggestions is to provide a range of options and opportunities to help inspire church members to make *The Year of the Bible* more than simply a one-time, one-year experience. Obviously, you want as many people as possible to continue reading the Bible on an ongoing basis. To accomplish that end, you will need to begin publicizing follow-up opportunities without delay.

Place an article in the church newsletter outlining an assortment of alternatives. At the same time, write a letter to all of the participants, summarizing the choices available and inviting them to become involved in one or more of these activities regularly.

The effort that you put into launching, sustaining, and concluding this program in the congregation will be well worth the time and energy it takes. Not only will you feel a strong sense of satisfaction, but many others will be energized and invigorated by the experience. Best wishes and God's blessings as you undertake *The Year of the Bible* in your congregation!

APPENDIX 1
SAMPLE MATERIALS FOR *THE YEAR OF THE BIBLE*

On the following pages are a number of items that will be of help as you engage in *The Year of the Bible* program. Notice that each of the materials lists the chapter and the page in the text to which it refers. As I have mentioned earlier, each of the samples is intended as a guide, and you should feel free to adjust them to your congregation's needs.

These are the materials that you will find in this appendix:

Sample A:	Groups and Individuals to Contact	Page 52
Sample B:	Sample Logo	Page 53
Sample C:	Versions of the Bible	Page 54
Sample D:	Advance Announcement: First Month	Page 55
Sample E:	Advance Announcement: Second Month	Page 56
Sample F:	Advance Publicity: Top Ten Reasons	Page 57
Sample G:	Bulletin Insert: Front Side	Page 58
Sample H:	Bulletin Insert: Back Side	Page 59
Sample I:	Newsletter Articles	Page 60
Sample J:	End-of-Year Newsletter Article	Page 61

GROUPS AND INDIVIDUALS TO CONTACT (Chapter 1, Page 10)			
Name of Group	Who to Contact	Date Contacted	Result of Meeting
Worship Committee			
Christian Education Committee			
Adult Bible Study Leaders/Teachers			
Choir Director and Music Leaders			
Youth Advisors			
Church Librarian			
Retreat Committee			
Women's Group			
Men's Group			

APPENDIX 1, SAMPLE A

SAMPLE MATERIALS FOR *THE YEAR OF THE BIBLE*

WESTMINSTER PRESBYTERIAN CHURCH

THE YEAR OF THE BIBLE

CURRENT YEAR

APPENDIX 1, SAMPLE B

VERSIONS OF THE BIBLE
(Chapter 1, Page 15)

Which Version Should I Read?

One of the first questions most people ask about participating in *The Year of the Bible* is what version of the Bible they should read. The first thing to say is that there is no one version that is best for all people!

A number of standard versions are available that will serve you well. There is the New Revised Standard Version (NRSV), which is a revision of the tried and true Revised Standard Version (RSV). Published in 1989, it promises to be the standard American translation for years to come. There is also the New International Version (NIV) and the Jerusalem Bible (JB). Like the NRSV, these translations are reliable, up-to-date, and fairly straightforward to read. If you like the more elegant style of British English, you may want to choose the New English Bible (NEB), also revised. Finally, the Good News Bible (GNB) is one to consider if you want to read a version that has a simpler, more colloquial style than the one that you normally use. This is a particularly good version for people for whom English is not their first language.

I would not recommend using the King James Version (KJV). Even though many people believe it is the most beautiful of all English translations and cannot be surpassed in its renditions of passages like the Twenty-third Psalm, its language is now antiquated. In addition, much more accurate translations (such as those mentioned above) are now available.

In spite of its popularity, I also would advise that you not use the Living Bible. It is very colloquial and can give a somewhat inaccurate translation of the meaning of the originals. One other version that is available is the New American Standard Bible (NASB). Unfortunately, it is not too helpful, because the translation employs a literal, almost wooden style.

What about a study Bible? If you are planning to buy a new version, I recommend that you consider getting one of these. You can get a study Bible in almost all of the major versions we have mentioned. They are not inexpensive these days, unfortunately, but the notes and comments in them are valuable in helping you to understand the text of the Bible better.

_____

(Pastor's Name)

APPENDIX 1, SAMPLE C

SAMPLE MATERIALS FOR *THE YEAR OF THE BIBLE*

ADVANCE ANNOUNCEMENT: FIRST MONTH
(Chapter 2, Page 22)

An Exciting Year Ahead

This coming year will be an exciting time for our congregation. We plan to make the Bible the theme for special emphasis during the entire year. This is the book that is basic to our faith. This is the book that has sustained millions and millions of people throughout their lives. This is the book that is special: it is God's Word to men and women.

Yet many people say that they do not know the Bible very well. We hope to change that next year! The [governing board] has adopted a program that we are calling *The Year of the Bible*. The centerpiece for the program is a challenge to everyone in the congregation *to read through the entire Bible in one year!* We will be providing help and guidance as the year progresses.

In December, the program will be explained in detail. This is a challenge and it will require commitment, but you will find the effort well worth your time. If you can't wait for more information or if you would like to help in planning for the program, give me a call.

_____

(Pastor's Name)

APPENDIX 1, SAMPLE D

ADVANCE ANNOUNCEMENT: SECOND MONTH
(Chapter 2, Page 22)

Next Year: The Year of the Bible

This coming year will be a special one in the life of our congregation. We are planning to give major emphasis to the Bible. It will be the focus of sermons, retreats, musical events, and many other activities in the life of the church.

The centerpiece for this emphasis on the Bible will be a call to everyone in our congregation to commit themselves to read through the entire Bible during the year. Many people say that they would like to know the Bible better, but they aren't sure how to go about doing that. Reading the Bible straight through is one way that seems to help many people. Those in our congregation who have done it in the past testify to how enjoyable and valuable the experience was for them.

It may sound like an imposing task to read the entire Bible in one year, but it can be done much more easily than you may suspect. It takes only fifteen to twenty minutes per day to do the readings. Of course, it will take some energy to plan reading time into your daily schedule. But even if you get behind on your reading occasionally, it is not that difficult to catch up.

It will be an exciting adventure as all of us together read through the pages of the Scriptures in this way. I am sure you will find this to be enriching and stimulating for your life as a Christian. I am looking forward to it. I hope you are too.

_____

(Pastor's Name)

APPENDIX 1, SAMPLE E

SAMPLE MATERIALS FOR *THE YEAR OF THE BIBLE*

ADVANCE PUBLICITY: TOP TEN REASONS
(Chapter 2, Page 22)

Top Ten Reasons to Sign Up for The Year of the Bible

10. Lots of other churches are doing it.
9. You can say you have read the Bible cover to cover.
8. It's more exciting than watching **The Simpsons**.
7. Everyone agrees that the Bible is important.
6. You'll know where to find Habakkuk.
5. Your congregation will experience a stronger sense of fellowship and unity.
4. It's cheaper than going out to buy another paperback novel.
3. How else will you read about God's gift to us in Jesus Christ?
2. It will help you "get into" the Bible.
1. The Bible is "a lamp to our feet and a light to our path."

APPENDIX 1, SAMPLE F

BULLETIN INSERT: FRONT SIDE
(Chapter 2, Page 24)

YOUR
LOGO
HERE

This is a special year in the life of [church name]. As an entire congregation, we will be setting out on an adventure together. We will be reading through the whole Bible in one year. Here is your chance to

- Read the entire Bible on a systematic basis
- Become familiar with the book that has influenced the lives of millions from ancient times to the present
- Draw strength and encouragement for your daily life
- Participate together with many in our congregation in a joint project with a common goal

The [governing board] has adopted *The Year of the Bible* as a primary emphasis for our church. We are encouraging all members to join in the readings. In fact, the officers and staff, as well as many others, have already committed themselves to participate in this program.

APPENDIX 1, SAMPLE G

SAMPLE MATERIALS FOR *THE YEAR OF THE BIBLE*

BULLETIN INSERT: BACK SIDE
(Chapter 2, Page 24)

Dear Friends in Christ,

The Bible will be the theme for the whole of [year] at [church name]. We have adopted the program *The Year of the Bible* to help us in this endeavor, and you will find the schedule of readings in the participant's book that goes with the program. We are asking you to make a commitment to read through the entire Bible during the year.

The readings will become the basis for many of the events in the life of our congregation next year. For instance, sermons will be based on the readings for the Sunday; adult education classes will discuss the passages for the week; musical events will take the Bible as their theme; and retreats will focus on the Bible.

As the year progresses, there will be a variety of suggestions and ideas that will help you to make your way through the readings so that by the end of the year, you will have read through the entire Bible!

From comments of people who have done this in the past, I am convinced that you will find *The Year of the Bible* to be a meaningful and rewarding program. Please fill out a card to indicate your intention to participate. You can obtain a participant's book in the [location].

Yours in Christ,

_____

(Pastor's Name)

"Your word is a lamp to my feet and a light to my path." (Ps. 119:105)

APPENDIX 1, SAMPLE H

NEWSLETTER ARTICLES
(Chapter 3, page 34)

If You're Behind

It is hard to believe, but we have heard that a few (only a *very* few people) have occasionally (only *very* occasionally) gotten behind in their readings. Since Leviticus, Numbers, and Deuteronomy are as gripping as any thriller novel, this is hard to imagine, but reliable informers say that it has occurred.

What can you do if you're behind, I mean, really behind? Well, don't give up. The best thing to do is to jump ahead and pick up the readings for the correct day again. That way, you will be with the rest of the group, and the various things in our congregational life (like the sermons!) will be more meaningful. Then, each day, try to add a little of the material you've missed. You will be surprised how quickly you can get caught up again.

Do You Have Questions About Your Readings?

Don't forget the question box on the resource table if you want to ask a question about your readings. We will answer (or, at least, try to answer!) your question, and it will be posted on the bulletin board by the table. Take some time to browse through the exhibits on the same table. They highlight the current readings and are provided courtesy of our own library.

APPENDIX 1, SAMPLE I

SAMPLE MATERIALS FOR *THE YEAR OF THE BIBLE*

END-OF-YEAR NEWSLETTER ARTICLE
(Chapter 4, page 46)

The End of the Year

Well, the year is over! Congratulations to all of you who were able to complete the course, reading through the entire Bible. I am sure there were any number of times when it was difficult to keep up with the three chapters or so of material a day, but I hope you have found the effort worthwhile.

In fact, quite a number of people have already said how valuable and meaningful the readings have been for them. That reminds me of the verse in Ps. 119:105: "Your word is a lamp to my feet and a light to my path." I'm glad that these words have proven true for so many of you, and I hope your experience this year has been an encouragement to continue with the Bible next year, and the next year, and beyond.

To help you continue making the Scripture part of your life, I am providing a variety of suggestions and plans for your use this coming year. You will find details about them on the resource table. Stop by soon to see what is available. I want to encourage you to use one of those or to use some other plan that will enable you to maintain a regular Bible study/devotional time in your schedule. We are all extremely busy, and some such plan can by very valuable in helping us to focus on our Lord and Savior in the midst of our hectic days and weeks.

Finally, I want to thank all of you who participated. A special word of appreciation to those who helped in various ways with organizing and carrying out the details of the program in our congregation. *The Year of the Bible* has been a unique and significant part of our life together. Thank you all!

_____

(signature)

APPENDIX 1, SAMPLE J

APPENDIX 2
WEEKLY BULLETIN QUESTIONS

In this appendix, you will find sample questions to include in the weekly bulletin. The purpose is to provide participants with specific material to look for as they do their readings during the week. In the following week's bulletin, along with questions for the next week, you should print answers to the previous week's questions. You will find an answer printed in parentheses following each question.

There is enough material included here to provide two or three questions for each week. As I mentioned in Chapter 3, I recommend that you write some of your own questions too. It is a challenge to develop clear, concise ones, but it is also enjoyable!

January 5	What does the rainbow after the flood symbolize? (The rainbow symbolizes God's covenant never again to destroy humanity with a flood.—Gen. 9:11–13)
January 5	Who were the two sets of brothers among the disciples? (Peter and Andrew, James and John are two sets of brothers among the disciples.—Matt. 4:18–22)
January 8	What is the reaction of Abraham and Sarah to the news that God will give them a son? (Abraham and Sarah both laugh at the idea that they will have a son.—Gen. 17:17; 18:12)
January 11	When Abraham was asked to sacrifice Isaac, who carried the wood? (Isaac carried the wood for his own sacrifice.—Gen. 22:6)
January 14	Jacob, the trickster, is himself tricked by Laban. How? (Laban switches daughters on Jacob, so that he is tricked into marrying Rachel's older sister, Leah.—Gen. 29:21–23)
January 16	While Jesus considers natural descent and family important, what is still more important? (Even more important than family or natural descent is doing God's will.—Matt. 12:46–50)
January 17	Jacob loses Rachel as she bears which of his twelve sons? (Rachel dies while bearing Benjamin.—Gen. 35:18)
January 17	What are the names of Jesus' brothers? (The brothers of Jesus were named James, Joseph, Simon, and Judas; we are not told the names of the sisters.—Matt. 13:55–56)
January 19	Shortly after being sold as a slave in Egypt, Joseph's position goes from bad to worse. Why? (Joseph ends up in prison because, insisting on being honorable and upright, he is falsely accused of immorality.—Gen. 39:20)
January 26	What does God tell Moses to say to the children of Israel when they ask the name of the God who sent him? (God instructs Moses to tell the children of Israel that the divine name is "I AM," or "I AM WHO I AM."—Ex. 3:14)

WEEKLY BULLETIN QUESTIONS

January 28	Was Aaron older or younger than his brother, Moses? (Aaron was three years older than his brother, Moses.—Ex. 7:7)
January 30	What Jewish group did not believe in a resurrection of the dead? (The Sadducees did not believe in a resurrection of the dead.—Matt. 22:23)
February 1	God provided for the children of Israel in the wilderness not only by giving them manna. What else did God give them for food? (God gave Israel quail as well as manna for food.—Ex. 16:13)
February 3	What does the eighth commandment prohibit? (The eighth commandment prohibits stealing.—Ex. 20:15)
February 5	Judas agrees to betray Jesus for what amount of money? (Judas betrays Jesus for thirty pieces of silver.—Matt. 26:15)
February 8	How many lambs were to be offered daily on the sacrificial altar? (Two lambs are to be offered each day on the sacrificial altar.—Ex. 29:38)
February 9	What does Moses do with the Ten Commandments when he finds the people worshiping idols at the base of Mt. Sinai? (When Moses finds Israel worshiping the golden calf, he breaks the tablets containing the Ten Commandments.—Ex. 32:19)
February 9	Name the person who is chosen to succeed Judas as one of the twelve apostles. (Matthias is chosen to succeed Judas as one of the twelve apostles.—Acts 1:26)
February 18	Which psalm may Jesus be quoting on the cross? (Jesus may be quoting from the opening words of Ps. 22 on the cross.—Matt. 27:46)
February 19	What very important prophetic passage is the man from Ethiopia reading when Philip finds him? (The Ethiopian is reading about the "Suffering Servant" in Isa. 53 when Philip finds him.—Acts 8:32–33)

February 20   On the Day of Atonement, when a goat is sent off into the wilderness or desert, what does it symbolically carry with it? (The goat sent into the wilderness on the Day of Atonement symbolically carries with it the iniquities of the people of Israel.—Lev. 16:22)

February 21   What does God wish to teach Peter with the vision of the clean and unclean animals? (Peter's vision of the clean and unclean animals shows him that God considers all human beings—both Jews and Gentiles—equal in God's sight.—Acts 10)

February 22   For what purpose does the Law tell people not to harvest their crops all the way to the edge of their fields? (The commandment not to harvest crops to the edges of the fields is intended to provide the poor with the possibility of obtaining food.—Lev. 19:9; 23:22)

February 26   Which tribe of Israel is given responsibility for the Tabernacle and its furnishings? (The tribe of Levi is given responsibility for the Tabernacle.—Num. 1:47–54)

March 2   How does Israel determine when to move to a new location in the wilderness? (Israel moves to a new location in the wilderness when the cloud no longer remains over the Tabernacle.—Num. 9:15–23)

March 3   In what city does Paul find an altar dedicated "To an unknown god"? (Paul finds an altar "To an unknown god" in Athens.—Acts 17:23)

March 4   Why is Miriam struck with leprosy? (Miriam is struck with leprosy because she, in jealousy, speaks against Moses.—Num. 12)

March 7   When a plague of serpents strikes the people as retribution for their sin, what does Moses do to bring them relief? (To save the people from the serpents, Moses sets up a bronze image on a pole.—Num. 21:4–9)

WEEKLY BULLETIN QUESTIONS

March 10   In Israel, could a father's inheritance ever pass to his daughters? (A daughter could receive her father's inheritance if there were no living sons.—Num. 27:8)

March 12   Who tips off the Roman authorities about the plot against Paul's life in Jerusalem? (Paul's nephew hears of a plot against Paul and informs the Roman authorities.—Acts 23:16–22)

March 14   What provision was made in the law for a person who killed another person accidentally? (To avoid retribution for killing someone accidentally, a person could flee to one of the "cities of refuge" designated by the law.—Num. 35)

March 16   Moses is permitted only to observe the Promised Land from a mountaintop. Who will lead the people when they enter it? (Since Moses may not enter the Promised Land, the people will be led into it by Joshua.—Deut. 3:23–28)

March 19   What situation is Paul in when the book of Acts ends? (When the book of Acts ends, Paul is under house arrest in Rome awaiting trial.—Acts 28)

March 22   What basic principle does the psalmist suggest for those who wish to have a long life? (The psalmist suggests that a primary way to secure a long life is to live a morally good life.—Ps. 34:12–14)

March 23   According to the Law, in cases where the death penalty is to be assessed, what persons are to take the lead in the execution? (In cases of the death penalty, the Law prescribes that the witnesses against the accused must take the lead in the execution.—Deut. 17:7)

March 24   Paul writes that Abraham is the ancestor of people who are linked to him not primarily by circumcision, but by what? (For Paul, Abraham is ancestor first of all of those who have faith.—Rom. 4:11–12)

March 27 While "the wages of sin" is death, according to Paul, what does God offer freely because of Christ? (The wages of sin is death, but God's free gift in Christ is eternal life.—Rom. 6:23)

March 31 Why does Moses climb to the top of Mount Nebo? (Moses climbs Mount Nebo to view the Promised Land before he dies.—Deut. 34:1–6)

April 1 What sign does Rahab use to indicate her house so that it will be spared when Israel takes Jericho? (Rahab ties a crimson cord in her window as a sign to the Israelites to spare her house when they take Jericho.—Josh. 2:18)

Romans 11:28-29 irrevocable.

April 3 Israel suffers after the fall of Jericho because of the sin of Achan. What does he do? (Achan sins by keeping some of the booty for himself.—Josh. 7:1, 21)

April 9 Who says "Choose this day whom you will serve, . . . but as for me and my household, we will serve the LORD"? ("Choose this day whom you will serve" is said by Joshua.—Josh. 24:15)

April 9 Paul writes that he hopes to visit Roman Christians after going to Jerusalem. Where does he want to go after he sees the Roman Christians? (After visiting the Roman Christians, Paul hopes to go on to Spain.—Rom. 15:24)

April 11 Normally in Israel, rulers and leaders were men. What important judge in Israel was a woman? (The important woman judge in Israel is Deborah.—Judg. 4—5)

April 11 What is especially noteworthy about the manner in which Jesus heals the leper? (It is especially significant that Jesus, in healing the leper, touches him with his hand, indicating God's love for one who is "untouchable."—Mark 1:41)

April 13 Which judge is asked to become king in Israel, but refuses, saying that the Lord is to rule over Israel? (Gideon tells the people that he will not be king because God should rule over Israel.—Judg. 8:23)

WEEKLY BULLETIN QUESTIONS

April 19	Some very special left-handers are mentioned in Judges. What is said about them? (Judges tells us about 700 left-handers who could hit a hair with a sling.—Judg. 20:16)
April 22	Who is Ruth's great-grandson? (Ruth's great-grandson is David, the king of Israel.—Ruth 4:17–22)
April 23	On the Mount of Transfiguration, which two figures from the Old Testament appear with Jesus? (At the Transfiguration, Moses and Elijah appear with Jesus.—Mark 9:4)
April 26	How does Saul show mercy shortly after becoming king? (Saul shows mercy by not taking revenge on those who had despised him when he was made king.—1 Sam. 10:27; 11:12–13)
April 27	From what book and chapter does Jesus quote when he is asked which commandment is greatest? (When Jesus is asked which commandment is greatest, he quotes from Deut. 6.—Mark 12:29)
April 30	Why does Saul become angry with David? (Saul is angry because the people praise David more than they do Saul.—1 Sam. 18:8)
May 4	Late in his life, a desperate Saul visits a medium at Endor to try to speak with someone who has died. Who? (Saul consults a medium at Endor in an attempt to speak to Samuel.—1 Sam. 28)
May 4	Paul often has colleagues working with him in his ministry. Who seems to be working with him when he writes 1 Corinthians? (Sosthenes is the colleague mentioned by Paul when he writes 1 Corinthians.—1 Cor. 1:1)
May 6	How does David respond when he learns that his mortal enemy, Saul, is dead? (When he gets news of Saul's death, David mourns him.—2 Sam. 1)

May 10 — What prophet is sent by God to confront David about his sin with Bathsheba? (The prophet who confronts David about his sin with Bathsheba is Nathan.—2 Sam. 12:1–15)

May 10 — Which psalm records David's prayer of confession because of the affair with Bathsheba? (Ps. 51 records David's prayer of confession following the affair with Bathsheba.)

May 11 — What does Paul think of lawsuits begun by Christians against other Christians? (Paul says that Christians should seek to solve grievances with the church, even to the point of being defrauded, rather than take each other to court.—1 Cor. 6:1–8)

May 19 — For what reason, according to Paul, has God given different gifts to different people within the congregation? (Paul says that God gives different gifts to different people for the common good, that is, to build up the congregation.—1 Cor. 12:7)

May 20 — What was contained in the Ark of the Covenant, according to 1 Kings? (1 Kings tells us that the two stone tablets were in the Ark of the Covenant.—1 Kings 8:9)

May 21 — When God judges Solomon by breaking up his kingdom, who is to become king of the ten tribes in the North? (When God divides the kingdom, Jeroboam, from the tribe of Ephraim, will become king of the ten northern tribes.—1 Kings 11:26–40)

May 22 — Why does Jeroboam set up altars for worship in Dan and Bethel? (Jeroboam sets up altars in Bethel and Dan to keep the people from making sacrifices in Jerusalem and, thus, probably becoming disloyal to him.—1 Kings 12:26–30)

May 23 — Paul tells us that when Jesus rose, he appeared specifically to two individuals. Peter (Cephas) is one; who is the other? (Paul tells us that Jesus appears not only to Peter individually, but also to James.—1 Cor. 15:7)

WEEKLY BULLETIN QUESTIONS 71

May 24   Who is the foreign woman married to Ahab, King of Israel? (Ahab's foreign wife is named Jezebel.—1 Kings 16:31)

May 29   That God cares for all people, not just the Israelites, is suggested by the fact that Elisha heals a foreigner from Syria. Who? (God's concern for foreigners is evident in Elisha's healing of the Syrian, Naaman.—2 Kings 5)

May 29   Paul speaks of a new covenant, not like the old covenant, which was based on the written law. What is the new covenant based on? (Paul speaks of a new covenant, based not on the written law, but on the Spirit.—2 Cor. 3:6)

June 1   Athaliah governs Judah for six years. What is unusual about this particular ruler? (What is unusual about Athaliah, who governs Judah for six years, is that this ruler is a woman.—2 Kings 11)

June 6   Sadly, Hezekiah, a good king, is succeeded by an evil son, Manasseh. What horrible thing does Manasseh do to one of his sons? (Hezekiah's evil son, Manasseh, sacrifices one of his own sons as an offering.—2 Kings 21:6)

June 6   What topic is Paul discussing when he says, "The one who sows bountifully will also reap bountifully"? (Paul is talking about financial stewardship when he says, "The one who sows bountifully will also reap bountifully."—2 Cor. 9:6)

June 7   The last king of Judah is taken captive to Babylon. What is his name? (Zedekiah, the last king of Judah, is carried off to Babylon as a captive.—2 Kings 25:7)

June 13   Usually Paul starts his letters by calling himself a "servant." This helps to emphasize his humility. What does he call himself in Galatians and what does this emphasize? (At the beginning of Galatians, Paul calls himself an "apostle" in order to emphasize his authority.—Gal. 1:1)

June 15 What reason does God give for having not David, but Solomon, build a temple, or "house," for God? (God has Solomon rather than David build the Temple because David has been involved in much warfare, while Solomon's reign will be characterized by peace.—1 Chron. 22:8–9; 28:3)

June 15 At Antioch, Paul confronts an important apostle who is avoiding eating with Gentile Christians because a group of Jewish Christians does not like the practice. Who is the apostle? (At Antioch, Paul confronts Peter, who is not eating with Gentile Christians because he fears the Jewish Christians who are opposed to the practice.—Gal. 2:11–13)

June 19 What are some of the things that Paul lists as examples of the "fruit" of the Spirit in a person's life? (The "fruit" of the Spirit in a person's life includes things like love, joy, peace, patience, kindness, generosity, faithfulness, gentleness, and self-control.—Gal. 5:22)

June 23 Paul says that Jesus' death makes peace possible between what two major groups of people? (Jesus' death makes peace possible between Jews and Gentiles.—Eph. 2:11–18)

June 25 What prophet tells Ahab that he will die in battle? (The prophet Micaiah tells Ahab that he will die in battle.—2 Chron. 18:18–22)

June 28 Which king of Judah is cursed by God with leprosy? (The king of Judah who is cursed by God with leprosy is Uzziah.—2 Chron. 26:19–23)

July 1 During the reign of which king is the Book of the Law rediscovered in the Temple? (During the reign of Josiah, the Book of the Law is rediscovered in the Temple.—2 Chron. 34:14)

July 2 Why are the people surprised when Zechariah names his son "John"? (The people are surprised when Zechariah names his son "John," because children were usually given a name belonging to someone else in the family.—Luke 1:61)

WEEKLY BULLETIN QUESTIONS

July 3	What king permits the Jews to return from Babylon to Judah? (Cyrus, the king of Persia, allows the Jews to return to Judah.—Ezra 1:2–4; 6:1–5)
July 6	Whose mother-in-law is healed by Jesus? (Jesus healed Peter's mother-in-law.—Luke 4:38–39)
July 8	What was the occupation of Nehemiah at the Persian court? (Nehemiah was the cupbearer to the king of Persia.—Neh. 1:11)
July 11	What information does Luke give us about Mary Magdalene? (Luke tells us that Mary Magdalene had been healed of seven demons.—Luke 8:2)
July 13	Which disciples accompany Jesus at the Transfiguration? (Peter, James, and John are with Jesus at the Transfiguration.—Luke 9:28)
July 15	Why does Haman wish to have all the Jews in Persia executed? (Haman wishes to have all Jews executed because Mordecai, a relative of Esther, refuses to bow down before him.—Esth. 3:1–6)
July 18	What Jewish festival is instituted in the Book of Esther? (The festival of Purim is instituted in the Book of Esther.—Esth. 9:20–26)
July 18	Does Jesus agree that the people who were killed when the tower of Siloam fell were worse sinners than other people? (Jesus does not agree that the people who were killed when the tower of Siloam fell were worse sinners than other people.—Luke 13:1–5)
July 19	Satan anticipates that, when everything is taken from Job, he will curse God. Does he? (Contrary to Satan's expectations, Job does not curse God when everything is taken from him.—Job 1—3)

July 24		What kind of person is the one leper who returns to thank Jesus for healing him? (The one leper who returns to thank Jesus for healing him is a Samaritan.—Luke 17:16)
July 27		What is the occupation of Zacchaeus? (Zacchaeus was a tax collector.—Luke 19:2)
August 1		When Jesus is dying on the cross, who affirms that he is innocent? (When Jesus is dying on the cross, a Roman centurion affirms that he is innocent.—Luke 23:47)
August 2		Job's "friends" insist that his sufferings must be due to some great sin or sins. Does Job admit their charges? (Job does not admit his friends' claim that his sufferings are due to his great sinfulness.—Job 31)
August 5		In what form does God appear to Job when God answers Job's questions? (God speaks to Job out of a whirlwind.—Job 38:1; 40:6)
August 6		Whom does Paul plan to send to the Philippians to bring back news about them? (Paul sends Timothy to get some news about the Philippians.—Phil. 2:19)
August 7		Does God conclude that Job or his friends are more accurate in what they have said about God's ways? (God concludes that Job has spoken more accurately about God's ways than Job's friends did.—Job 42:7)
August 7		What Jewish tribe does Paul belong to? (Paul comes from the tribe of Benjamin.—Phil. 3:5)
August 10		Why does Paul give thanks for the church at Colossae? (Paul thanks God for the faith and the love of the Colossians.—Col. 1:3–4)
August 14		What was the occupation of Luke? (Luke was a physician.—Col. 4:14)

[handwritten margin note near July 27: "Usher's Psalm 84:10"]

WEEKLY BULLETIN QUESTIONS

August 16	What psalm does the devil quote in tempting Jesus to throw himself down from the pinnacle of the temple? (In tempting Jesus to throw himself down from the pinnacle of the temple, the devil quotes Ps. 91.—Matt. 4:6)
August 18	Who did Paul send to Thessalonica to find out how the church he had founded was faring? (Paul sent Timothy to see how the church at Thessalonica was faring.—1 Thess. 3:2)
August 22	Proverbs mentions four things that are small, but wise. What are they? (The four small, but wise, things mentioned in Proverbs are ants, badgers, locusts, and lizards.—Prov. 30:24–28)
August 27	According to Ecclesiastes, why is a living dog better off than a dead lion? (Ecclesiastes says that a living dog is better off than a dead lion because it still participates in this life.—Eccles. 9:4–6)
August 27	Paul cherished a deep affection for Timothy. How does Paul describe his relationship to him? (Paul feels so close to Timothy that he looks at him as his child.—1 Tim. 1:2, 18)
August 29	When all is said and done, what is the basic thing that people should do, according to Ecclesiastes? (Ecclesiastes says that, when all is said and done, the basic thing people should do is fear God and keep the commandments.—Eccles. 12:13)
September 3	Isaiah complains that the people of Judah are not even as wise as an ox. Why? (Isaiah complains that Israel is not as wise as an ox, because an ox at least knows to whom it belongs.—Isa. 1:3)
September 3	What is the root of all kinds of evil, according to Paul? (Paul says that the root of all kinds of evil is the love of money.—1 Tim. 6:10)
September 4	Who was Timothy's grandmother? (Timothy's grandmother was Lois.—2 Tim. 1:5)

September 5	In what chapter is Isaiah's vision of God's holiness and his call to be a prophet recorded? (Isaiah's vision of God's holiness and his call to be a prophet is recorded in Isa. 6.)
September 10	Where was Titus when Paul wrote to him? (When Paul wrote to him, Titus was on the island of Crete.—Titus 1:5)
September 13	How long will the psalmist sing praises to the Lord? (The psalmist will sing praises to the Lord as long as he lives.—Ps. 104:33)
September 14	What was the name of Philemon's runaway slave who had become one of Paul's helpers? (Philemon's runaway slave who had become one of Paul's helpers was named Onesimus.—Philem. 10)
September 17	According to Hebrews, how has Jesus as a high priest been made like believers in every way? (According to Hebrews, as a high priest, Jesus has been made like believers in that he both suffered and was tested.—Heb. 2:18)
September 19	Who prays for deliverance from Sennacherib because this seemingly invincible Assyrian king has mocked the "living God"? (Hezekiah prays for deliverance from Sennacherib, the Assyrian king, because he has mocked the "living God."—Isa. 37:17)
September 22	What Persian king does God, in a prophecy of Isaiah, call "my shepherd"? (God calls the Persian king Cyrus "my shepherd."—Isa. 44:28)
September 24	Hebrews tells us that Jesus is a priest along the lines of what mysterious Old Testament figure from the time of Abraham? (Hebrews calls Jesus a priest along the lines of the mysterious Old Testament figure Melchizedek.—Heb. 6 and 7)
September 28	In Isaiah, God's word is compared to rain and snow. Why? (Isaiah compares God's word to rain and snow which, when they are sent forth, accomplish their task successfully.—Isa. 55:10–11)

WEEKLY BULLETIN QUESTIONS 77

September 28   According to Hebrews, what cannot possibly take away sin? (Hebrews says that the blood of bulls and goats cannot possibly take away sin.—Heb. 10:4)

September 30   Like Proverbs, what does Ps. 111 say is the beginning of wisdom? (Like Proverbs, Ps. 111 says that the "fear of the Lord is the beginning of wisdom."—Ps. 111:10)

October 2   Where do you find the famous verse, "Jesus Christ is the same yesterday and today and forever"? (The famous verse, "Jesus Christ is the same yesterday and today and forever," is found in Heb. 13:8.)

October 3   Who asks, "Can anything good come out of Nazareth?" (Nathanael asks, "Can anything good come out of Nazareth?"—John 1:46)

October 7   When Jesus says that the Temple has become a den of robbers, what prophet is he quoting? (When Jesus says that the Temple has become a "den of robbers," he is quoting Jeremiah.—Jer. 7:11)

October 10   In connection with what miracle performed before a multitude does Jesus say, "I am the bread of life"? (In connection with the feeding of the 5,000, Jesus says that, "I am the bread of life."—John 6:35, 48)

October 12   Who seeks to protect Jesus by pointing out that a person should not be judged without a hearing? (Nicodemus seeks to protect Jesus by pointing out that a person should not be judged without a hearing.—John 7:51)

October 13   Angered by Jeremiah's prophecies, what does the priest Pashhur do to him? (Angered by Jeremiah's prophecies, the priest Pashhur beats him and puts him in stocks.—Jer. 20:2)

October 17   A major problem in Israel was knowing which "prophets" were truly bringing God's word. Which prophet disagrees with Jeremiah's prophecies about Nebuchadnezzar? (Hananiah, "the prophet from Gibeon," disagrees with Jeremiah's prophecies about Nebuchadnezzar.—Jer. 28)

October 17   To whom does Jesus say, "I am the resurrection and the life"? (Jesus says to Martha, "I am the resurrection and the life."—John 11:25)

October 19   Who comes to Philip saying, "Sir, we wish to see Jesus"? (Some Greeks say to Philip, "Sir, we wish to see Jesus."—John 12:21)

October 28   Which is the longest psalm? (Ps. 119 is the longest psalm. Congratulations, you have just finished it!)

October 28   Who is the Babylonian king at the time Zedekiah, the last king of Judah, is carried off into captivity? (At the time Zedekiah is carried off into captivity, Nebuchadnezzar is king of Babylon.—Jer. 52:4)

October 29   One of the Scriptures cited in Handel's *Messiah* is "Look and see if there is any sorrow like my sorrow." Where does it come from? (The words in Handel's *Messiah* "Look and see if there is any sorrow like my sorrow," come from the book of Lamentations.—Lam. 1:12)

October 29   Who helps Joseph of Arimathea bury Jesus? (Nicodemus helps Joseph of Arimathea bury Jesus.—John 19:39)

October 30   What does "doubting Thomas" call Jesus when he sees him after the resurrection? (Upon seeing Jesus after the resurrection, Thomas calls him, "My Lord and my God!"—John 20:28)

October 31   In what country is Ezekiel living when he receives his initial, amazing vision? (Ezekiel is living in Chaldea, or Babylonia, when he receives his initial, amazing vision.—Ezek. 1:1–3)

November 3   What two Old Testament figures does James point to as he insists that works must accompany faith? (In insisting that works must accompany faith, James points to Abraham and Rahab.—James 2:21–25)

WEEKLY BULLETIN QUESTIONS

November 6 — Which writer recommends that our long-range planning should keep in mind the saying, "If the Lord wishes"? (James recommends that our long-range planning should keep in mind the saying, "If the Lord wishes."—James 4:15)

November 7 — Which two Old Testament people does James mention as examples of patient endurance and effective prayer? (James mentions Job and Elijah as examples of patient endurance and effective prayer.—James 5:11, 17)

November 14 — To what does Peter compare the elders in the church? (Peter compares the elders in the church to shepherds.—1 Peter 5:1–5)

November 18 — Where do you find the vision of the dry bones? (The vision of the dry bones is found in Ezek. 37.)

November 19 — If you found some of the things in Paul's epistles difficult to understand, you may enjoy especially a comment in 2 Peter 3. What is it? (If you found some things in Paul's epistles difficult to understand, you may enjoy the fact that in 2 Peter 3:16 it says the same thing about them.)

November 23 — According to 1 John, anyone who hates his brother can be compared to what Old Testament character? (1 John 3:11–15 says that anyone who hates his brother is like Cain, whose hatred led to murder.)

November 24 — In Ezekiel's vision of a new temple and new city of Jerusalem, what does he say the city will be called? (In Ezekiel's vision of a new temple and new city of Jerusalem, he says that the city will be called "The Lord is There"—Ezek. 48:35.)

November 25 — Why does Nebuchadnezzar have Shadrach, Meshach, and Abednego thrown into the fiery furnace? (Shadrach, Meshach, and Abednego are thrown into the fiery furnace by Nebuchadnezzar because they will not worship an idolatrous image.—Dan. 3:13–23)

	November 30	What is the name of Hosea's unfaithful wife? (Hosea's unfaithful wife is named Gomer.—Hos. 1:2–3)
	November 30	Whose brother is Jude? (Jude calls himself the "brother of James," which is probably a reference to the James who was the brother of Jesus.—Jude 1:1; see Matt. 13:55)
	December 1	Where was John when he received the message of Revelation? (John was on the island of Patmos when he received the message of Revelation.—Rev. 1:9)
	December 6	Which psalm affirms that the Lord knows all about us, wherever we are? (Ps. 139 affirms that the Lord knows all about us, wherever we are.)
	December 7	What is John told when he weeps because no one is worthy to open the scroll sealed with seven seals? (When John weeps because no one is worthy to open the scroll sealed with seven seals, he is told not to weep because Jesus Christ can open the scroll.—Rev. 5:5)
	December 10	In Amos, God says that he wants nothing to do with Israel's festivals, assemblies, offerings, and worship because the people are lacking two highly important things. What are they? (In Amos, God says that he wants nothing to do with Israel's festivals, assemblies, offerings, and worship because the people are lacking justice and righteousness.—Amos 5:21–24)
	December 11	What does John see when the Lamb opens the seventh seal? (When the Lamb opens the seventh seal, John sees seven angels with seven trumpets standing before God.—Rev. 8:1–2)
	December 15	What reason does Jonah give for fleeing to Tarshish rather than going to Nineveh as God had commanded him? (Jonah explains that he fled to Tarshish because he knew that God was gracious, and therefore he feared that God would forgive the people of Nineveh if they repented.—Jonah 3:10—4:2)

WEEKLY BULLETIN QUESTIONS

December 17   In what chapter of what book is the birth of Jesus in Bethlehem foretold? (The birth of Jesus in Bethlehem is foretold in Mic. 5.)

December 18   In Micah we read that what God considers good—what the Lord requires of us—is essentially three things. What are they? (According to Micah, what God considers good and requires of us is to do justice, to love kindness, and to walk humbly with God.—Mic. 6:8)

December 18   According to Revelation, the "mark of the beast" is a name, represented as a number, which people will be forced to bear if they hope to participate in trade and commerce. What is the number? (The number of the beast, the name which everyone will have to bear to participate in trade and commerce, is "666."—Rev. 13:18)

December 20   Which chapter of what prophet is the source of the quotation used by Paul, "The righteous live by their faith"? (The quotation used by Paul, "The righteous live by their faith," comes from Hab. 2:4.)

December 28   The Gospel of John quotes the words, "They look on the one whom they have pierced," at the crucifixion of Jesus. From which prophet does John take the quotation? (The quotation in the Gospel of John at the crucifixion, "They look on the one whom they have pierced," comes from Zech. 12:10.)

December 29   Why will there be no temple in the new Jerusalem? (There will be no temple in the new Jerusalem because the Lord God and the Lamb will themselves function as the temple, that is, the place where God and human beings meet.—Rev. 21—22)

December 31   Which prophet tells us that a messenger will be sent to prepare the way before the appearance of the Lord? (Malachi tells us that a messenger will be sent to prepare the way before the appearance of the Lord.—Mal. 3:1)

NOTES